Cleopatra Butterfly
Gonepteryx Cleopatra

Blue Pansy
Precis Orythia

Hercules Beetle
Dynastes Hercules

Chalk Hill Blue
Polyommatus Coridon

Fiery Butterfly
Acraea Acrita

2-Spot Lady Beetle
Adalia Bipunctata

Honey Bee
Apis Mellifera

Madagascar Giant Swallowtail
Papailio Antenor

15 Spot Lady Beetle
Anatis 15-Punctata

Forest Mother-of-pearl
Salamis Parhassus

D0551345

Darwin very much enjoyed observing and collecting insects.
Test your skills at being a naturalist by using the insect chart
on the end pages to find and identify some of the
beetle and butterfly species inside the book.

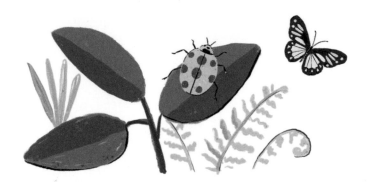

PUFFIN BOOKS

UK | USA | Canada | Ireland | Australia
| India | New Zealand | South Africa

Puffin Books is part of the Penguin Random House group of companies
whose addresses can be found at global.penguinrandomhouse.com.

www.penguin.co.uk   www.puffin.co.uk   www.ladybird.co.uk

 Penguin
Random House
UK

First published 2019
001

Printed in China
A CIP catalogue record for this book is available from the British Library

ISBN: 978–0–141–38850–2

All correspondence to:
Puffin Books, Penguin Random House Children's
80 Strand, London WC2R 0RL

CHARLES DARWIN'S

On the
ORIGIN
of
SPECIES

Retold and illustrated
by Sabina Radeva

PUFFIN

A long, long time ago, before humans even existed, the living world looked very different from how it looks today. Since life on Earth began, tiny organisms, plants and animals have been changing slowly, over millions of years, because of a process we call evolution.

For most of human history, many people believed that everything in the world was created all at once. They thought that plants, animals and people were always the same as they are now.

But there were a few clever and curious scientists around who challenged this idea.

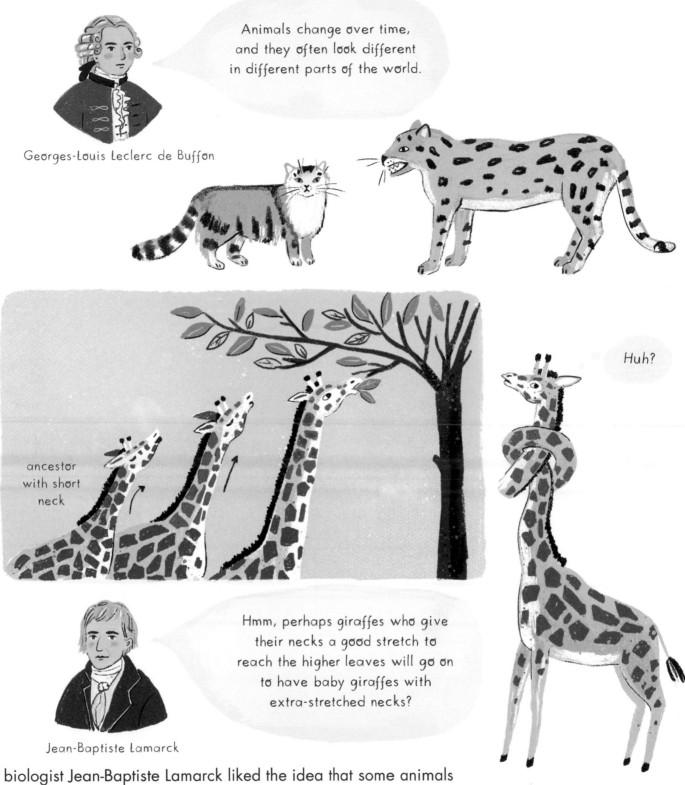

Animals change over time, and they often look different in different parts of the world.

Georges-Louis Leclerc de Buffon

ancestor with short neck

Huh?

Hmm, perhaps giraffes who give their necks a good stretch to reach the higher leaves will go on to have baby giraffes with extra-stretched necks?

Jean-Baptiste Lamarck

French biologist Jean-Baptiste Lamarck liked the idea that some animals evolved by using certain body parts more than others. It turned out he was a little off the mark with that theory, but it certainly did get people thinking!

✳ See Appendix VI

It was right to notice that living things changed – or evolved – over time, but nobody was quite sure *how* this happened.

Soon though, the world came to know Charles Darwin, an English naturalist who would change people's understanding of how different species came to be.

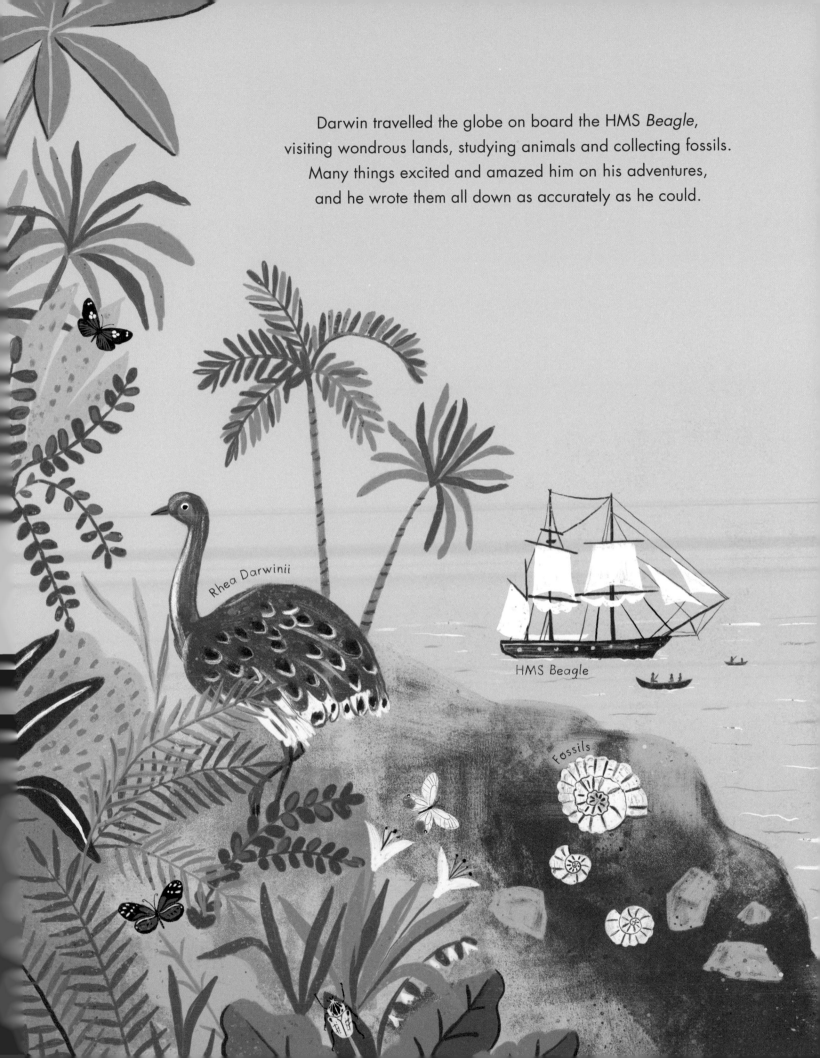

Darwin travelled the globe on board the HMS *Beagle*,
visiting wondrous lands, studying animals and collecting fossils.
Many things excited and amazed him on his adventures,
and he wrote them all down as accurately as he could.

Rhea Darwinii

HMS Beagle

Fossils

Down House

The Darwin Family

Charles Robert Darwin

Emma Wedgwood

William Erasmus

Anne Elizabeth

Henrietta Emma

George Howard

Elizabeth

Francis

Leonard

Horace

Polly

When Darwin returned from his expedition, he worked from his English country house, where he lived with his wife, eight children, and his dog Polly!

But Darwin had another long and difficult journey ahead. He had a new, big idea he wanted to share with everyone but, to explain it, he would have to do a lot of writing, studying and discussing with other scientists.

Darwin liked to study the orangutan Jenny at London Zoo.

The greenhouse was one of Darwin's favourite spots. He conducted many intriguing experiments there.

See Appendix 1

In 1859, after 20 years of hard work, Darwin was finally able to publish his book, *On the Origin of Species*, which explained all of his ideas.

In his book, Darwin explains that **species** are groups of living things that look alike and can have babies together. But even if they belong to the same species, no two animals are *exactly* the same.

Look closer and you will see some are:

TALLER

SHORTER

"*I look at the term species, as one arbitrarily given for the sake of convenience to a set of individuals closely resembling each other*"

FASTER

SLOWER

or different in
COLOUR!

These differences are known as variations.

Poodle

Bloodhound

Pug

English Pointer

Variation under Domestication

Italian Greyhound

Bulldog

Animals that people have tamed and domesticated, like pets and farm animals, look very different from their wild ancestors. Take man's best friend for example – we now have over 340 breeds of dog! People have raised them for their different sizes, shapes, colours and even talents. Yet all of these breeds came from one kind of wild wolf, many howling moons ago!

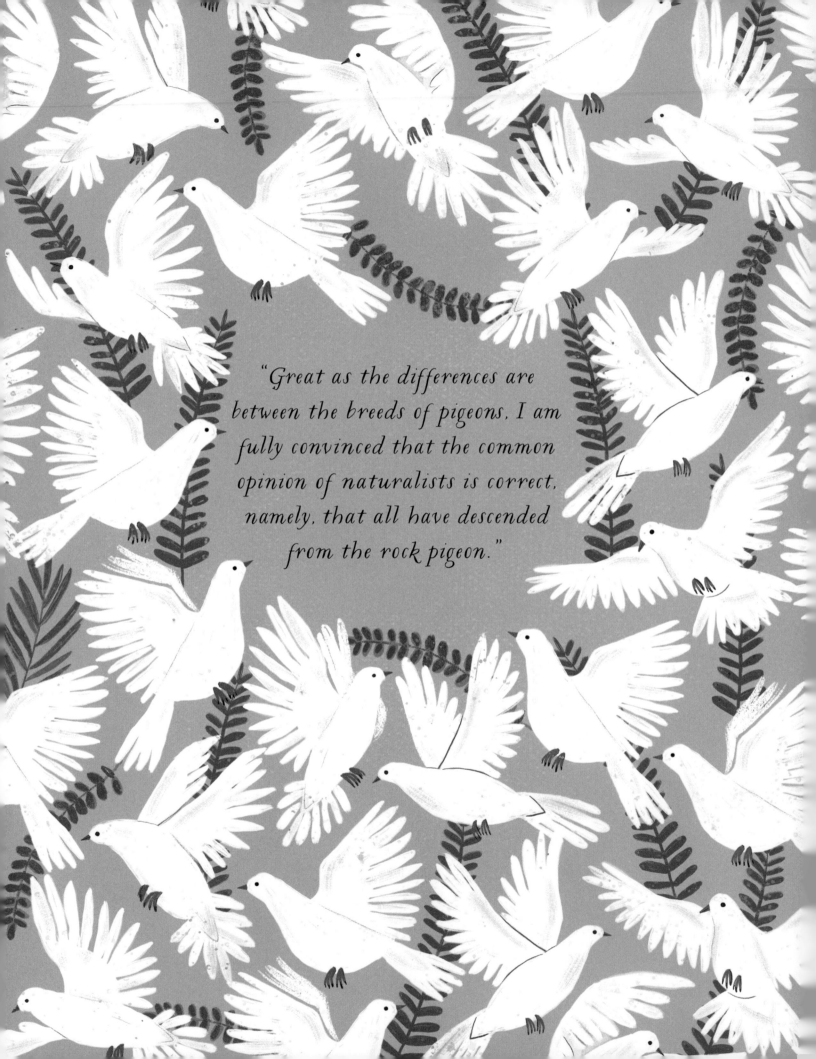

"Great as the differences are between the breeds of pigeons, I am fully convinced that the common opinion of naturalists is correct, namely, that all have descended from the rock pigeon."

Columba Livia or Rock Pigeon

Fantail

English Pouter

Short-Faced Tumbler

English Carrier

Scandaroon

English Barb

Trumpeter

Jacobin

Frillback

Darwin studied pigeons too. Just like dogs, Darwin knew that all pigeons belong to the same species, although you certainly wouldn't think so to look at them!

Gardeners may encourage the growth of
plants with large and beautiful flowers
while they might weed out those that
don't quite make the grade.

Like pets, farm animals and even garden flowers can look very different from their wild ancestors. This is mostly because people make choices. Farmers may choose to breed the cows that produce the most milk, the chickens that lay the best eggs, and the sheep with the warmest and most knittable wool.

Variation under Nature

Species change in the wild too. Even without human influence of any kind, plants sprout and young animals in the wild are born, all with slight differences. Some differences don't matter, some are not helpful at all . . .

Oh dear, perhaps two heads aren't always better than one.

. . . but some differences are very useful.

Darwin noted that Galapagos finches have developed beaks in all sorts of shapes and sizes. These differences help them to pick up their favourite snacks. Different beaks are good for different nibbles.

Large beak for crushing tough seeds

Small beak for feeding on soft seeds

Long and sharp beak helps to tear cactus flowers

Beak that can hold tools to probe and find insects

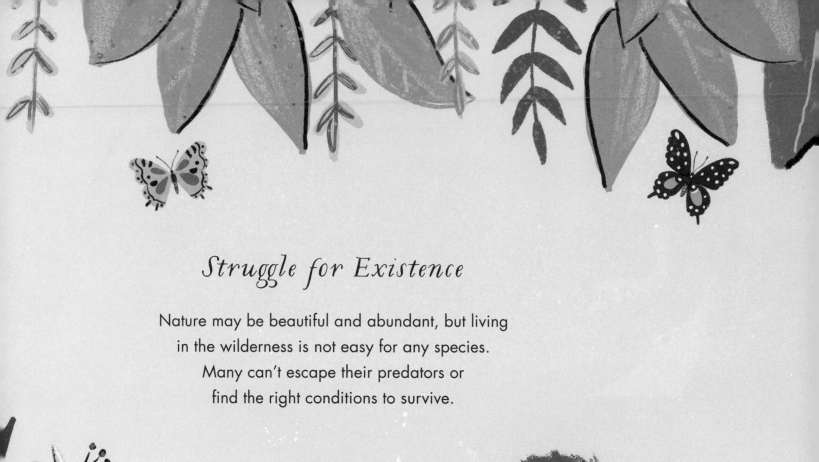

Struggle for Existence

Nature may be beautiful and abundant, but living
in the wilderness is not easy for any species.
Many can't escape their predators or
find the right conditions to survive.

"Every organic being naturally increases at so high a rate, that, if not destroyed, the earth would soon be covered by the progeny of a single pair."

Animals compete for food and shelter – things they must have if they are to survive and have babies. It's a struggle to live in the wild and only the best adapted will succeed.

"I estimated that the winter of 1854-55 destroyed four-fifths of the birds in my own grounds."

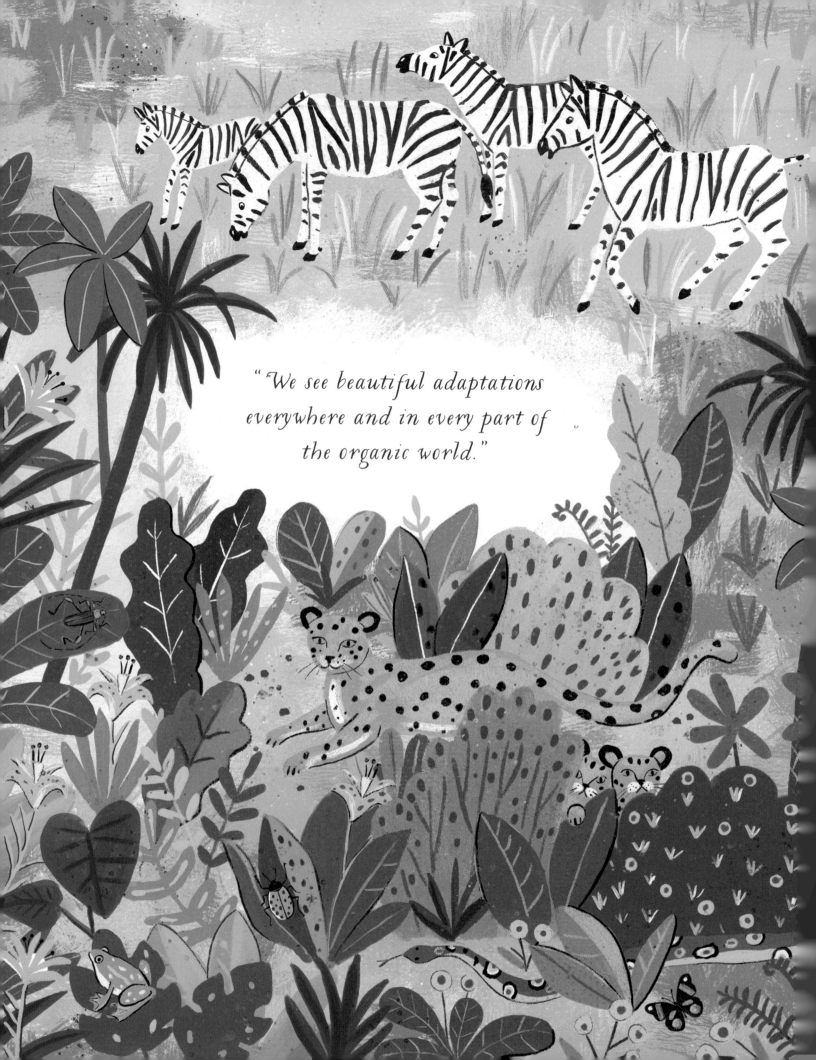

"We see beautiful adaptations everywhere and in every part of the organic world."

Natural Selection

Some differences help animals survive in the wild. Some help them to hide, to hunt, to live longer or have lots of babies. Those babies will then grow to benefit from the helpful differences that have been passed down from their parents. The species is adapting to the world around it.

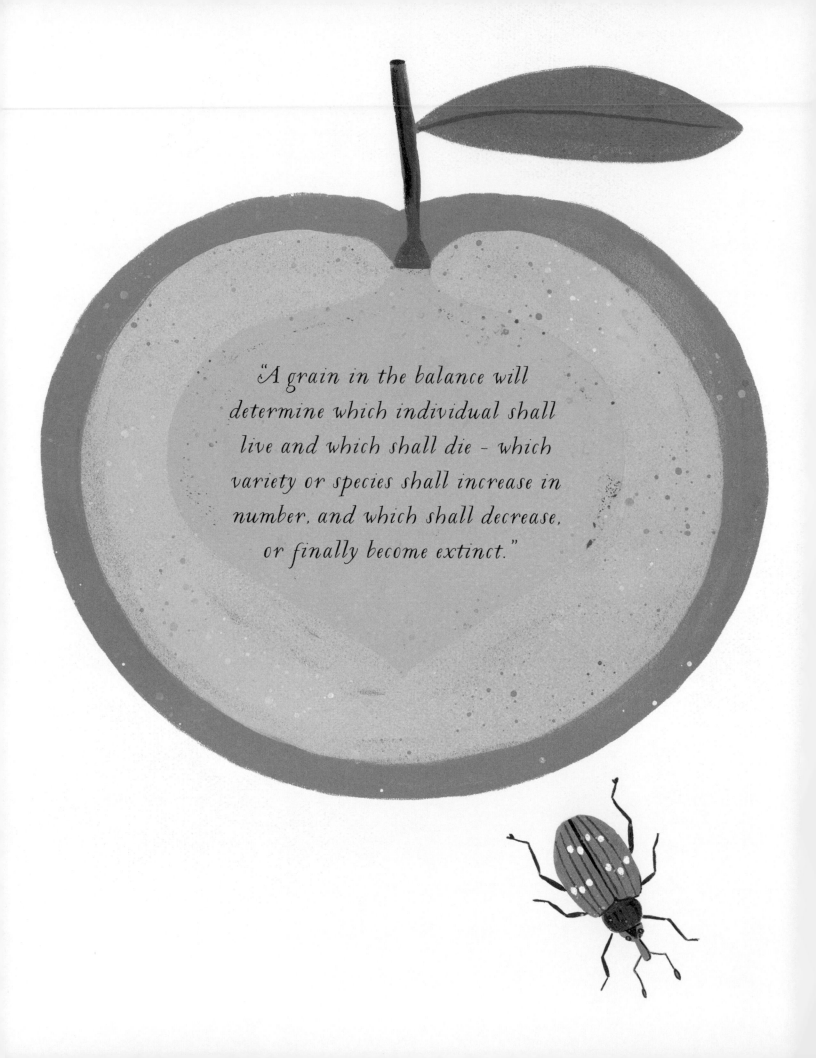

"A grain in the balance will determine which individual shall live and which shall die - which variety or species shall increase in number, and which shall decrease, or finally become extinct."

Even small differences in colour or design can help an animal or plant to live, survive and reproduce better. Darwin called this **Natural Selection.**

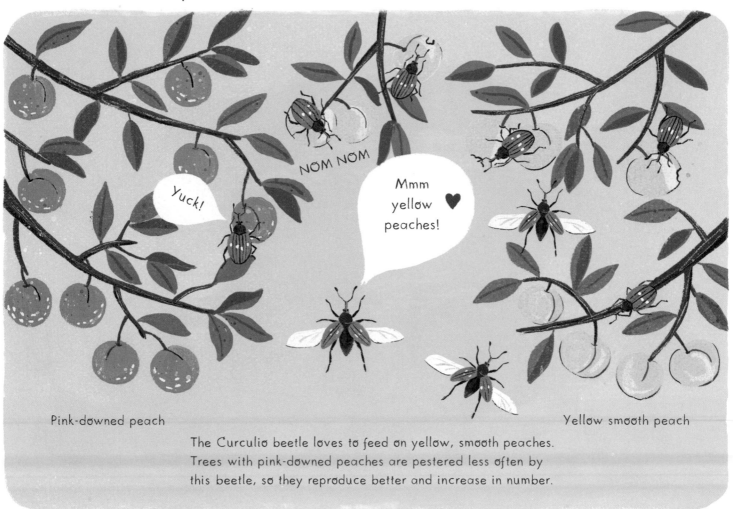

Pink-downed peach

Yellow smooth peach

The Curculio beetle loves to feed on yellow, smooth peaches. Trees with pink-downed peaches are pestered less often by this beetle, so they reproduce better and increase in number.

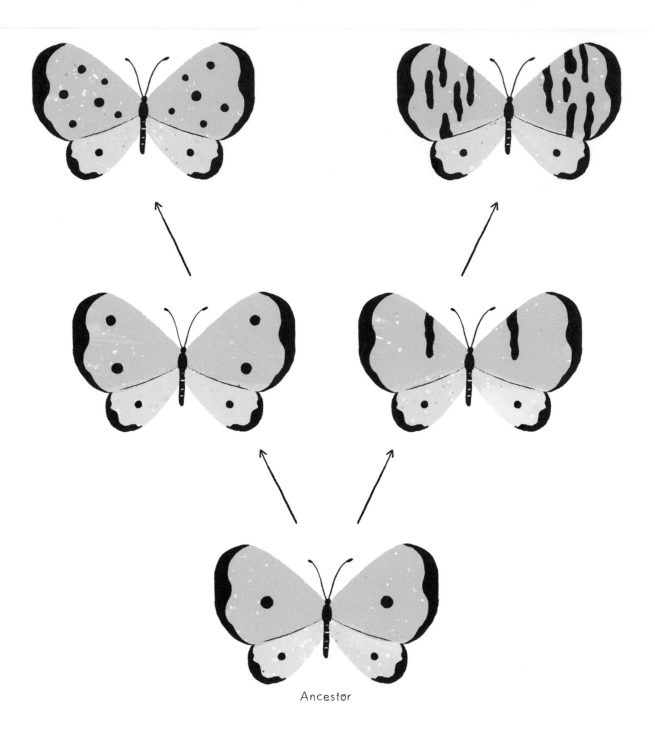

Ancestor

Over a really long time, these little differences can add up and a species can change so much that they become a whole new species. Darwin suggested that this is a really slow process, taking tens of thousands of years. That's why it's hard to see evolution happening with our own eyes!

Of course just as new species form, others die out or become extinct.

✳ See Appendix IV and V

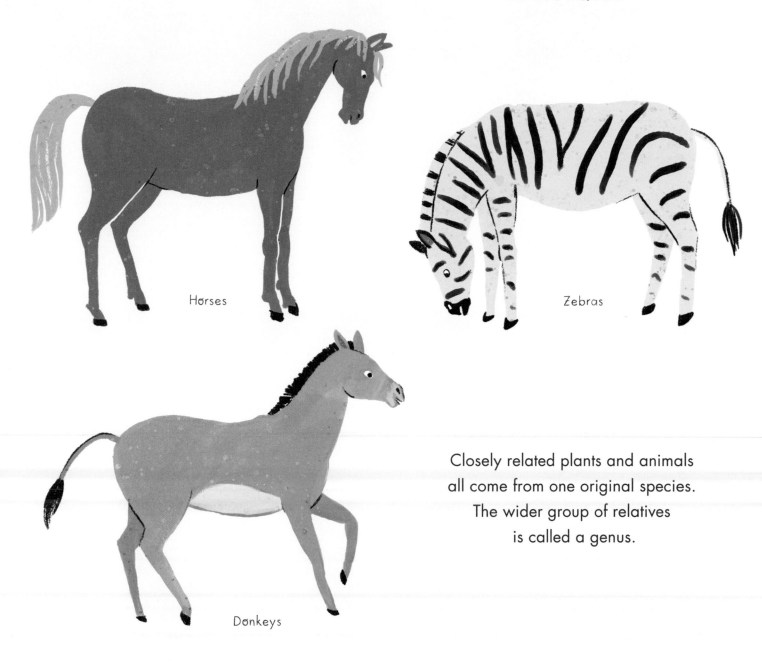

Horses

Zebras

Donkeys

Closely related plants and animals
all come from one original species.
The wider group of relatives
is called a genus.

Sometimes features that seem to have
vanished forever can suddenly reappear.
For example, some Devonshire ponies
are born with stripes just like zebras,
which suggests they may share
a stripy common ancestor!

"As buds give rise by growth to fresh buds, and these, if vigorous, branch out and overtop on all sides many a feebler branch, so by generation I believe it has been with the great Tree of Life, which fills with its dead and broken branches the crust of the earth, and covers the surface with its ever branching and beautiful ramifications."

Darwin drew a picture of a tree to show how species evolve. Scientists have taken this idea even further and shown that humans, animals, plants, insects and even the tiniest creatures are all descended from the first living things that ever came to be.

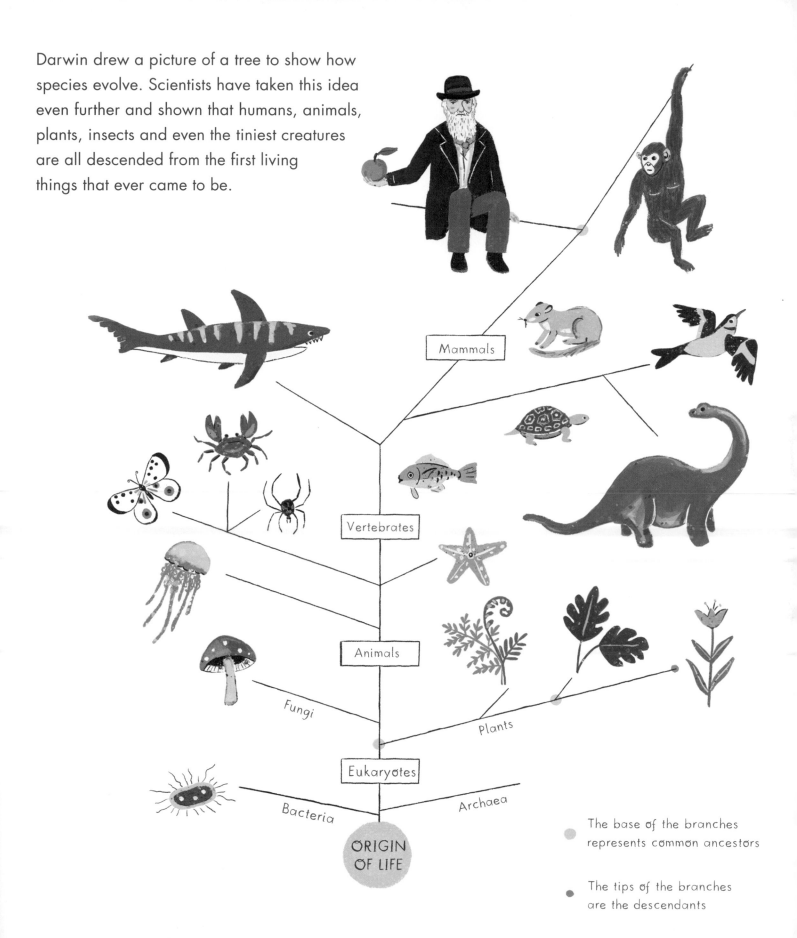

Mammals

Vertebrates

Animals

Fungi

Plants

Eukaryotes

Bacteria

Archaea

ORIGIN OF LIFE

The base of the branches represents common ancestors

The tips of the branches are the descendants

So how did life begin? Where did it first come from? Darwin wasn't sure, but his theory explains how it evolved into the many living things we see on planet Earth today.

"Why, if species have descended from other species by insensibly fine gradations, do we not everywhere see innumerable transitional forms? Why is not all nature in confusion, instead of the species being, as we see them, well defined?"

Difficulties on Theory

Darwin knew that his theory was difficult to prove, and that people would ask questions about it. His book is filled with answers to those questions – for example: if species gradually change over time, why do we not see many in-between forms, in the middle of all these changes?

Darwin explained that Natural Selection makes living things better adapted to where they live. Once animals with more useful traits appear, they will compete and replace those that are less adapted.

"The crust of the earth is a vast museum"

Fossils are evidence of extinct species – like dinosaurs, woolly mammoths and the Dodo bird – but there weren't many fossils to show species as they were changing. Darwin explained that this is because perfect conditions are needed for fossils to form, and those conditions are pretty rare.

Imperfections of the Geological Record

As rocks get bashed by the wind and sea, they break down into pieces called sediment.

sediment

When animals die and get covered in layers of sediment, like a blanket, they can be preserved in sedimentary rocks.

soft sediment

compact

But the chances of this happening are very small indeed, so we'll never know just how weird and wonderful many extinct species might have been!

"Can we believe that natural selection could produce, on the one hand, organs of trifling importance, such as the tail of a giraffe, which serves as a fly-flapper, and, on the other hand, organs of such wonderful structure, as the eye, of which we hardly as yet fully understand the inimitable perfection?"

Organs of Extreme Perfection

EVOLUTION OF THE EYE

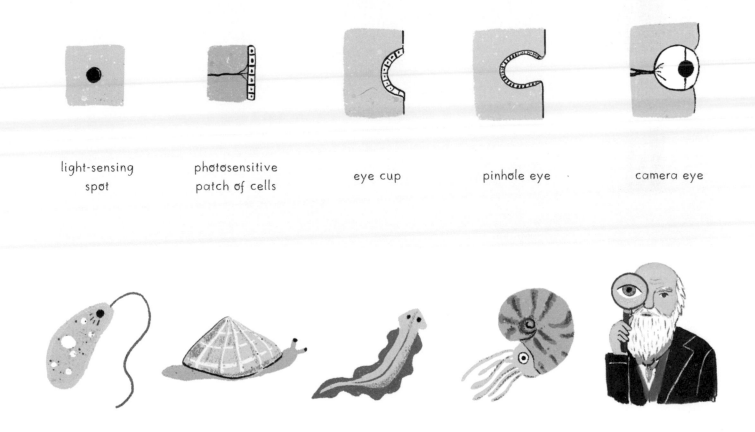

| light-sensing spot | photosensitive patch of cells | eye cup | pinhole eye | camera eye |

According to Darwin, animals become more complicated as they evolve and new body bits are made from the old designs, rather than being started from scratch. Very complex organs like eyes evolved from what were simple designs to begin with. The eye was formed by tiny changes and upgrades over millions of years.

120°

"What shall we say to so marvelous an instinct as that which leads the bee to make cells, which have practically anticipated the discoveries of profound mathematicians?"

Instinct

Natural Selection doesn't just focus on how creatures look, but also on how they behave. Instinct is the seemingly magical way an animal is born knowing how to work with its environment. For example, many birds somehow know they must travel to warmer places during winter; and honey bees create perfect hexagon shapes in which to store their honey, without ever being taught. These are examples of instincts and, if an instinct helps an animal to survive better, it can be kept and passed on to future generations.

Mountains, rivers and seas create natural barriers to migration, and many animals have difficulty crossing oceans.

Plant seeds can be carried or eaten by birds and 'deposited' later, allowing them to spread more easily. This is why plants around the world often seem similar, but animals in different places are more different!

MIGRATION

MIGRATION

ancestor species

Darwin explained how species spread around the world by something called migration. New species that start in one place will sometimes move to other places. In their new environment, the species will often change even more.

Migration

Because they are surrounded by water and cut off from the mainland, islands have become home to some of the most unusual animals on the planet. One BIG example of these unusual animals, spotted by Darwin, was a giant tortoise in the Galapagos Islands.

Pinta

GALAPAGOS ISLANDS

Isabela

Hood

Florena

It is thought that an ancestor of that tortoise floated to the island. With no predators or other large plant-eaters to compete with for food, the tortoise did very well for herself, as did her descendants. So far, evolution has caused the giant tortoise to get bigger and bigger over time, and it now weighs in at over 250kg.

250kg (550 pounds)

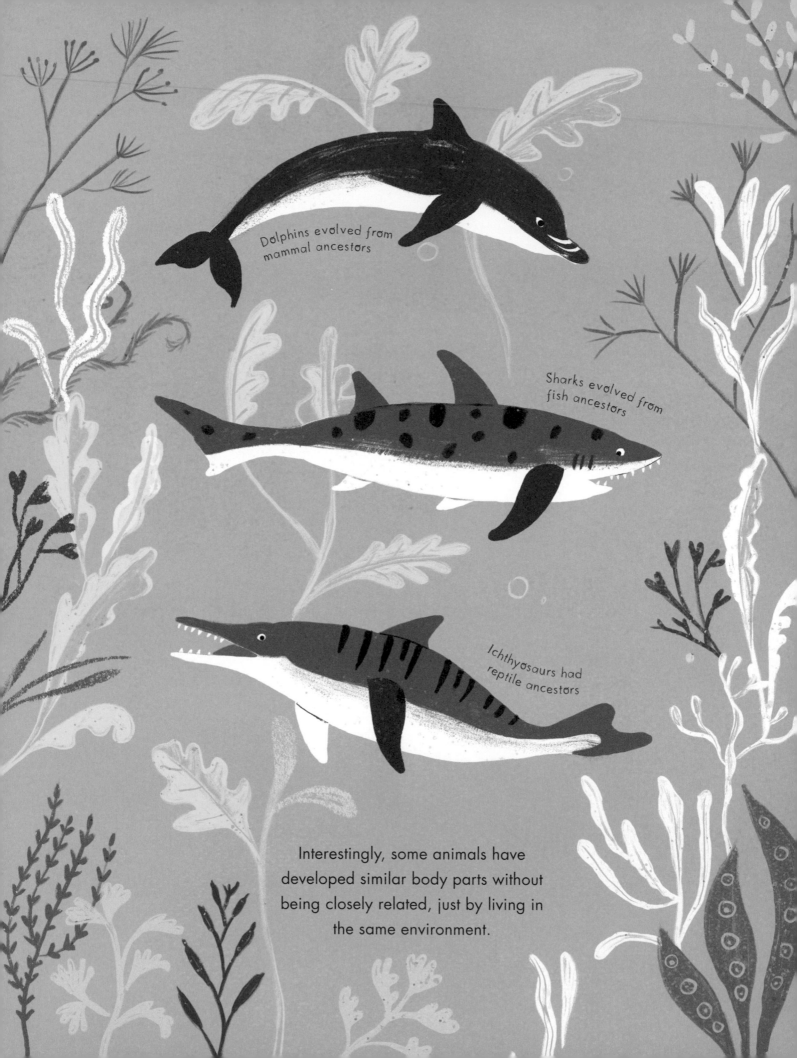

Dolphins evolved from mammal ancestors

Sharks evolved from fish ancestors

Ichthyosaurs had reptile ancestors

Interestingly, some animals have developed similar body parts without being closely related, just by living in the same environment.

whale fin

bat wing

dog paw

frog leg

human hand

lemur leg

"From the first dawn of life, all organic beings are found to resemble each other in descending degrees, so that they can be classed in groups under groups."

Naturalists usually rely on the insides and bones to find out if species are really related. For example, many species share the same five-fingered bone structure in their hands, paws or flippers. This points to a shared branch in the tree of evolution.

Before any animal is born or hatched, it is a tiny being called an embryo. At the very first stages, some embryos are quite difficult to tell apart. These similarities go to show that all animals are related at some level. Each creature has evolved its own different features based on the same basic blueprint for a creature's beginnings here on Earth.

✳ See Appendix VIII

Indohyus

Pakicetus

Ambulocetus

Dorudon

rudimentary
hind leg bones

Many animals have bones, organs and other parts which don't do anything any more, but were very important for their ancestors. Because they don't harm the animal's chance of survival, these leftovers haven't disappeared even though they're no longer of any use. From the remains of our own lost tails to the leftover leg bones from a whale's time walking upon the land, our bodies tell the history of our evolution.

"*In the distant future I see open fields for far more important researches . . . Light will be thrown on the origin of man and his history.*"

"Whilst this planet has gone cycling on according to the fixed law of gravity, from so simple a beginning endless forms most beautiful and most wonderful have been and are being evolved."

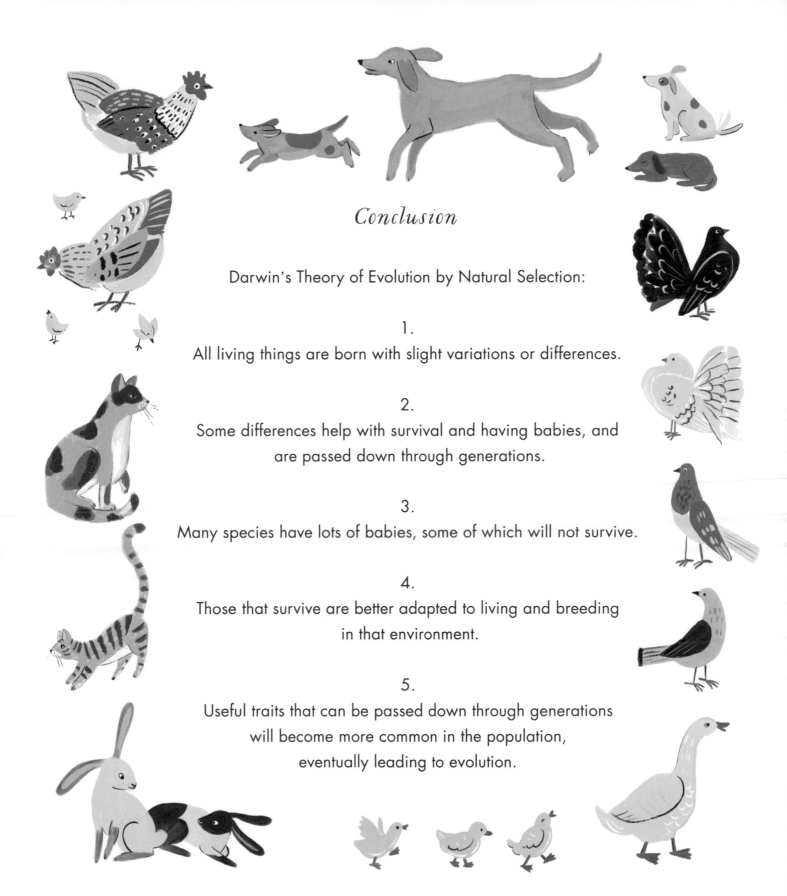

Conclusion

Darwin's Theory of Evolution by Natural Selection:

1.
All living things are born with slight variations or differences.

2.
Some differences help with survival and having babies, and
are passed down through generations.

3.
Many species have lots of babies, some of which will not survive.

4.
Those that survive are better adapted to living and breeding
in that environment.

5.
Useful traits that can be passed down through generations
will become more common in the population,
eventually leading to evolution.

Darwin's book comes to an end, but the process of evolution keeps going. For as long as the cycle of life goes on, we will adapt and evolve alongside our fellow animals and plants, here on planet Earth.

Author's Note

Dear reader, I have attempted here to create a faithful picture-book adaptation of *On the Origin of Species* by Charles Darwin. From this book children can learn the power of observation and recognize how curiosity about the natural world can lead to incredible discoveries. In the absence of modern technology (on which science nowadays relies a little too much), Darwin was able to conduct enough credible research to transform our understanding of life on Earth.

There was a lot of fascinating information to cover so I wasn't able to include much of his journey on HMS *Beagle*. For those fans who are eager to see more of the journey depicted I have recommended in the end notes some excellent picture books that can complete your Darwin collection.

With our ever-increasing modern knowledge it came to pass that certain aspects of the original text are outdated. Where this is the case I have endeavoured to include the up-to-date scientific information in the Appendix. It is also worth noting that when compiling *On the Origin of Species*, Darwin carefully avoided any speculation on the human origin, probably to avoid even further controversy at the time. Later he dedicated *The Descent of Man* to this topic.

Appendix

I. **Alfred Wallace** was another British scientist who developed a theory similar to Darwin's. This encouraged Darwin to finally finish his book. Their work was published together in one paper in 1858. Darwin spent longer developing his theory and as a respected naturalist he became known as the father of the evolutionary theory.

Alfred Russel Wallace

II. DNA and Genes

All living things are made of tiny units called cells. Most cells contain a code carried on a molecule called DNA. It looks like a spiralling ladder, a shape known as a double helix. Within each string of DNA are sets of instructions. The genetic code carries all the information that decides what a living thing will grow up to be like.

DNA

Cell

III. Inheritance

To inherit something means it has been passed down to you from your parents, grandparents, great-grandparents and so on. Inheritance in genetic terms is the way a living thing looks or behaves, and how that is passed down through generations. Our unique design is determined by the genes we inherit from our parents.

Parent   Children

IV. Variation and Mutations

Darwin still didn't quite know everything about inheritance or how variations occur in order to be passed to the next generation. Now we know that DNA drives evolution. Sudden changes in genes are called mutations. Sometimes mutations alter the way a living thing looks or functions and such mutations are the reason variations exist.

Mutated DNA

Cold Environment

Steppe Mammoth

Woolly Mammoth

V. Natural Selection

Darwin thought evolution by Natural Selection was gradual and ongoing. However, every so often, a new mutation has had a big impact and allowed species to evolve very quickly. Major environmental changes, such as ice ages, have also sped up evolution, as animals race to adapt to new challenges.

Starving Parent

Babies may store more fat to survive harsh conditions

VI. Epigenetics

Scientists have found that lifestyles and habits can affect the expression of genes without directly changing their code. These effects can also be passed to offspring. A starving animal may produce babies who store more fat from their food, for example. We still don't completely understand the mechanisms of epigenetics, but we know Jean-Baptiste Lamarck was not completely wrong about his theory that changes based on an animal's lifestyle can be passed down to new generations.

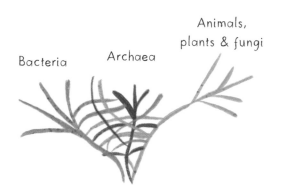
Bacteria   Archaea   Animals, plants & fungi

VII. The Tangled Thicket of Life

Darwin sketched a tree-like picture to explain the origins and relationships of species. However, new findings show that occasionally DNA can move between branches from species to species, through viruses carrying DNA for instance. This has led many scientists to insist that the Tree of Life should look more like a tangled shrub.

VIII. Comparative Embryology

In early years scientists like Ernst Haeckel wrongly proposed that all embryos repeat stages of evolution and all embryos look identical at the very first stages of development. This theory was disproved. Nowadays modern science shows that species that have similar embryonic development are closely related and probably have a common ancestor.

Misconceptions

Evolution explains the origin of life on Earth

No, this is a misconception (a mistaken belief). The theory of evolution does not explain how life on Earth started. Darwin's theory explains how species can change over time, and how new species are created from existing species, by the process of Natural Selection.

Evolution proves that we evolved from monkeys

No, humans did not evolve from monkeys as we know them now. All primates shared a common ancestor some 25 to 30 million years ago, and both monkeys and humans evolved from this animal in lots of different ways, until we became the species we are today. Modern primates, like monkeys and apes, are more like cousins. You are descended from your parents but you are only related to your cousins.

Evolution is when one kind of animal gives birth to another kind of animal

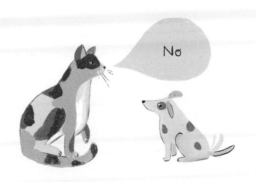

No, an individual animal can never give birth to a completely new kind, or new species of animal. For example, a cat will never give birth to a dog. Instead, young animals are born with small differences, and after many generations the species gradually changes.

You can't see evolution happening

You can sort of, but evolution is a very slow process that takes thousands of years. In a human lifetime we can only see a snapshot of the creation of a new species. However, in the laboratory scientists have been able to see how bacteria, plants and fruit flies mutate and change. In the wild many insects have built up a resistance to pesticides and when we see these changes we are observing evolution.

Human Lifetime

Glossary and Recommended Literature

Adapt
To modify or adjust to new conditions or a new environment

Adaptation
A special feature or way of behaving that helps a living thing to survive

Ancestor
An earlier form of an animal or plant from which the others have evolved

Descendant
A living thing that has descended from a particular ancestor

DNA
The substance that carries genetic information within the cells of all living things

Evolve
To change or develop very gradually over time

Extinct
Species no longer in existence, no longer having any living members

Fossil
The ancient remains of an animal or plant preserved in layers of rock

Generation
A group of plants or animals born and living in the same period of time

Genes
Small sections of DNA, which together determine the characteristics of a living thing

Genus
A group of related species of plants or animals

Naturalist
A person or scientist who studies and appreciates nature

Offspring
The children or young of a specific parent, or parents

Primates
A large and diverse group of mammals including humans, apes and monkeys

Sediment
Small pieces of rocks/soil that have come away, they sink and settle in layers

Species
A group of animals or plants that are similar and can produce offspring together

Variation
A slightly different version of something, distinct from other similar lifeforms

Recommended Reading
There are some wonderfully informative books on the topic of evolution that you might enjoy for further reading.

Grandmother Fish by Jonathan Tweet and Karen Lewis
The Tree of Life by Peter Sís
What Mr Darwin Saw by Mick Manning and Brita Granström

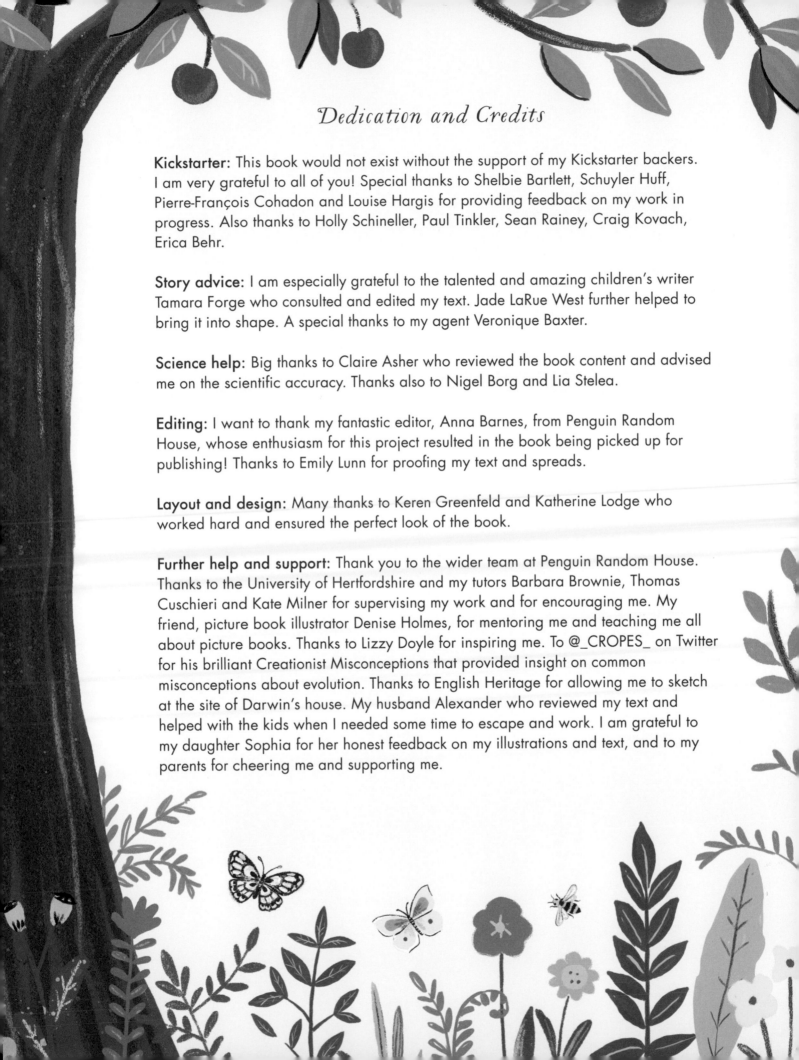

Dedication and Credits

Kickstarter: This book would not exist without the support of my Kickstarter backers. I am very grateful to all of you! Special thanks to Shelbie Bartlett, Schuyler Huff, Pierre-François Cohadon and Louise Hargis for providing feedback on my work in progress. Also thanks to Holly Schineller, Paul Tinkler, Sean Rainey, Craig Kovach, Erica Behr.

Story advice: I am especially grateful to the talented and amazing children's writer Tamara Forge who consulted and edited my text. Jade LaRue West further helped to bring it into shape. A special thanks to my agent Veronique Baxter.

Science help: Big thanks to Claire Asher who reviewed the book content and advised me on the scientific accuracy. Thanks also to Nigel Borg and Lia Stelea.

Editing: I want to thank my fantastic editor, Anna Barnes, from Penguin Random House, whose enthusiasm for this project resulted in the book being picked up for publishing! Thanks to Emily Lunn for proofing my text and spreads.

Layout and design: Many thanks to Keren Greenfeld and Katherine Lodge who worked hard and ensured the perfect look of the book.

Further help and support: Thank you to the wider team at Penguin Random House. Thanks to the University of Hertfordshire and my tutors Barbara Brownie, Thomas Cuschieri and Kate Milner for supervising my work and for encouraging me. My friend, picture book illustrator Denise Holmes, for mentoring me and teaching me all about picture books. Thanks to Lizzy Doyle for inspiring me. To @_CROPES_ on Twitter for his brilliant Creationist Misconceptions that provided insight on common misconceptions about evolution. Thanks to English Heritage for allowing me to sketch at the site of Darwin's house. My husband Alexander who reviewed my text and helped with the kids when I needed some time to escape and work. I am grateful to my daughter Sophia for her honest feedback on my illustrations and text, and to my parents for cheering me and supporting me.

ABOUT THE AUTHOR

Sabina Radeva is a graphic designer and illustrator based in London, England. In 2008 she graduated from the Molecular Biology M.Sc. programme at the Max Planck Institute, Germany.
In 2009 she left science for a creative career, and she has since studied as an illustrator. Sabina is passionate about projects that blend science with art. She is the mother of two little girls that are her source of daily inspiration. Beautifully illustrated, her retelling of *On the Origin of Species* was an immediate sensation around the world when launched on Kickstarter – and it is now her first published book!

Blue Fungus Beetle
Gibbifer Californicus

Ulysses Butterfly
Papilio Ulysses

Jewel Beetle
Temognatha Spencii

Blue Spot Pansy
Junonia Westermanni

Queen Alexandra's Birdwing
Ornithoptera Alexandrae

Lycid Beetle
Trichalus Ampliatus

Yellow Glassy Tiger
Parantica Aspasia

Adolias Imperator
Lexias Satrapes

Goliath Beetle
Goliathus Albosignatus

Five-bar Swordtail
Graphium Antiphates

Last's Albatross
Appias Lasti

Zigzag Beetle
Erotylus Incomparabilis